Contents

Spirit Affair

(Scenario: walking along the seashore at evening time)

Tomorrow, the Lord and I will talk and walk together, hand in hand.

Each step I take, I feel His warm embrace drawing me closer and closer to His heart. His heart is where I want to be. I'm safe to tell Him how much I've missed Him.

My mind races back to those precious moments, an intimate encounter where we touch each other. My desire to please Him overrides my fears to leave Him, so I look into His eyes; they are my assurance to go ahead.

His eyes gently follow my mind as if He knows its destination. The tone of His voice to urge me on says, "I want you to know me. I know you better than yourself. Don't be afraid, I made you. Your happiness is in knowing Me."

I hold His hand a little tighter now as I'm about to let Him feel my heart. I'm afraid because it's all torn up. I don't want anyone, not even God to see how broken down it really is. So I shamefully say, "it hurts, it hurts... I don't know why!"

While contemplating my vulnerability, I can sense His concern is a house of refuge. But somehow I suddenly blurt out, "Yes, I know... this happened, that happened, one thing after another. The pressures of trying to survive disaster have left me desolate, miserable and unhappy. All of this has passed, but the aftermath still lingers on." So in my mind, I humbly ask if there is a slight chance to live again because my hope is to love in a fresh, new way.

I cry and cry and cry as though He understands the meaning of every fallen tear. Louder and louder the sounds of pain, hurt, anguish and fear all line up, taking their turn to show and tell Him what agony I've suffered.

I turn toward Him, in front of Him and lay myself on the altar of His love. Pure love is wonderful, it never asks for anything in return. You can undress your image, cast the mask aside for you'll not need it anymore when you've found true love. As I lay on His treasure chest of mercy and grace, I cry again that I've found someone to unload the cares of this life.

As I draw close to Him, I find strength to wrap my arms around His neck. Oh, I feel so good inside. But wait, in the silence of His embrace I think about my future. I want it, but there's a gulf of fear and failure; the past that separates me from what I wish to be.

"Oh Lord I need help, I need your help. Please help me. I'm afraid of this, of that… how, when, where?" In my mind, I storm the universe for unequivocal answers; I'm convinced my embryonic hopes have been destroyed.

As He calls my name, quietly He whispers in my ear, "shh-shh-shh, I'm here, I'm right here; I'm your answer. There's no need to panic about your future. It's just You and Me."

As He gently rocks me from side to side to the melodious sounds of *You and Me*, I can feel His healing touch, like warm oil drip into the tenderness of my soul.

His heart is so clear to me now. He's doing what He does best - loving me in spite of my past, unconditionally. Alas, I've found someone who can bury the trash and restore the treasures of my heart.

At this point my arms have collapsed from His embrace, and I've put my entire body into His strong arms.

In His arms, He has miraculously brought the past, present and future to personalize our time together.

The past He dispels, the present He smiles upon, the future we walk, hand in hand, heart to heart; we create a dream together - His Will.

My Heart's Desire

(Interpretation of tongues)

O, how my heart longs to be with Thee;
the riches of your kindness draws
me closer each day to Thee.

Your awesomeness I find impeccably true;
Your presence so holy.

Holy, holy; I bow down in spirit
and worship You alone;
For You alone do things wonderfully,
creatively, subtly,
both large and small.

I worship and appreciate your goodness in men's lives;
for it is when I see your handiwork,
I humble myself.

When your throne of glory is revealed,
I see with my own eyes
the light of your countenance.

My mind cannot begin to remember all the
mercies You've shown, but my spirit can.

O, what joy it is to have You, Lord;
I appreciate your kindness towards men.

For Thy sake only do I hope to live;
You are the reason that causes me to want to live.

My soul cannot help but rejoice when You show such good favor towards
me; although I don't deserve it;
it's simply because You've chosen me.

Your chosen, You cherish.
Your chosen, You love.

Your chosen, You protect.
Your chosen, You never neglect.

My Prayer:

Please be my help and rid me from Egypt's past;
for it is dead, but not buried
and reeks with sorrow.

Help me, dear God to bury the dead;
I long for newness, a freshness to
behold You in new ways and times.

O God, give me direction and strength
to bring me into that place of promise,
the land of promise, my Canaan.

Seal me with peace;
make with me a covenant of peace
as You did with Phinehas,
the son of Eleazar,
Aaron's son, the priest.
[Numbers 25: 11-12]

And let not the sins of my forefathers
steal my future;
for whom You have blessed,
no man can curse.

Structure my life that I may do your will to inherit the promise; for riches,
wealth and honor belong to the righteous.

And I know that in this, You will prove yourself,
and show me how great and mighty You are.
[Jeremiah 33:3]

Precious Moments

How wonderful and pleasant it is to feel
your sweet lips roam the pastures of my soul.

I reach to wrap myself around your
sheer garment of power and majesty.

My ears are ever so tender to hear your voice;
my eyes are filled with the rain of your love.

O Lord, I yearn to be in your presence,
just to sit and never remove myself;
I find no other satisfaction than in being with You.

I'm weakened by your love,
yet strengthened because You love me.

It is your love that fights for me;
your love that heals all my wounds
both great and small, within and without.

Your love woos me to rest in your presence;
the delicacies of my heart anoints your feet -
even they are most holy, indeed.

I sit as a child enthralled by your presence on the ground of your heart and
find a place of comfort and strength as I rest my head alongside your legs,
leaning into an embrace
as I talk about You and I - just the two of us.

You, O God, are too much for me to behold;
but if I live for a long time, maybe I will have beheld just a glimpse of your
glory -

For You show up in many ways not numbered.

Everlasting Love

God, sometimes I can't seem to talk to You.

I choke with tears; my heart breaks
melting the wall of fear.

I can feel your sweet breath cover my body,
blowing and creating something anew within.

Though I search my finite mind,
my logic has failed me for some basis,
some reason, some clue of an inkling of why.

Why You love me!?!
Better yet, why You chose me?

God says to me,
"You'll never find the reason
because there isn't one.
'Why' doesn't exist beyond my love;
because I have loved you with an
everlasting love."
[Jeremiah 31:3]

My Personal Visit

You send a gentle, warm breeze
and kiss my lips with sunshine.

I reach out to embrace the wind of your love;
your comfort I can't let go.

My heart sinks in desperation
to express my love returned.

Your skirt of glory sweeps over me;
I faint at your awesomeness.

Since a thousand years is as one day,
what I longed for many years is
experienced in one moment.

So I smile upon the promised lifetime
of fulfillment I now have.

Overwhelmed and filled with joy;
I'm speechless, indeed, that
God comes and talks with me.

Sweet Innocence

I thrive on your touch wanting it more and more.

I scream inside from the excitement of You being near me. I can feel You smile at me. I can feel You laugh with me. We're having a good time. I'm glad we're alone, just me and You - You and I, us two. What a combination. I never thought it would happen.

Tears well up in my eyes at this surreal experience. Sometimes it seems too good to be true and I say something silly like, "God, am I getting too personal with You?" And You say, "Ha, I made you. You couldn't hide anything from Me if you tried. I created you, knowing more about you than yourself, unless I reveal it."

My response is: O God, You're just too much for me to handle. You are my life and my joy. Thank you God for giving me an opportunity to reveal myself, express myself, to stretch my imagination in love - pure, true love alone.

I can be naked with You; I feel no shame. My body is one with You, the Creator; there's no fear of how I respond to You.

So I lay prostrate, unclothed, waiting for You to breathe on me. I can feel You caress my heart with hands so soft I melt inside, yet firm that You hold me tight and secure.

My mind wonders in amazement, "How can You do that? Just how can You!?"

In gentleness, You seize and capture my thoughts, while pressing into my heart until the verge of falling apart is quite near.

My Lord, your holiness flatters me to no end; I can't help myself. In my own strength, I try to drive away addiction but it grips me tighter, more and more, each time.

Dear God, I look forward to our future together, and may I be good pleasure to You, as You have been to me.

Find Comfort in Me, Confide in Me

Come, come here, my Lord and
rest your head on my lap.

Come, come to a place where
You can tell me your heart.

I know You carry alot of things inside;
running the universe,
attending to men's needs
can be quite burdensome.

I want You to rest awhile, stay here with me;
I'll hold You and take You for mine.

If I could, I'd hide You from
the evilness of this world.
Sometimes, I wish people would do right by You,
even your people too.

I'm sick of how men treat You. I must hold You,
squeeze You, comfort You upon my breast.

Share with me your hidden treasures,
and cause me to know your mysteries.
Delight to know my soul, my King
and unveil yourself to me;
I'll tenderly protect your deepest secrets,
trust me.

I'll be your friend to the end. I'd die for You!
I won't leave You. I can't, I just can't -
my soul is tied to Thee.

Here, let me rock You in my arms
and sing You a lullaby;

one that will make You smile
and your coming worthwhile.

Enjoying the Moment

One day I'll have a family to enjoy the holidays;
days filled with fun, noise and laughter.

Although I have a pretty good glimpse of what a family entails (the 2nd oldest
of 11 children),
it's not quite like having your own.

Right now, I'm enjoying my singlehood;
God is such good company - more than enough.

His presence is ever abiding and resting in me,
what a special treat to enjoy day by day.

I know when that time comes,
I'll look back and smile on these days;
thanking Him for giving me such a
divine opportunity to be alone,
to share myself with Him.

Sometimes, I get a little concerned that
I'll have to give up our closeness for marriage.
But He says to me, "You'll just be loving Me
in a different way - through people I have so
carefully chosen to enrich your life."

It is during these holidays when I look
ten years into time and cherish the
moments with God I have yet remaining.

Can We Make it Last

Coming in from a hard day's work, somewhat not feeling well today. I
know if I can just get home where your peace dwells in abundance, I'll be
relieved.

I can take off my burdens and cares of the day, my personal struggles and
toils will become obsolete. For You are now the foremost existing force that
engulfs me with pleasure.

O, it is so quiet here. No one could have done this but You, brought me to a
place so spacious, warm and peaceful.

O, I love it. I want it to last forever. I'm not married yet, but it's in these
tranquil times
I often and quite honestly ask myself,
"How long will it last?"

I want to hold on to the fragrance of the wind that blows through my
bedroom window;
I know God sends it just for me.

He sends a chirping bird by to call my name,
the sweet charm of melody it sings.

I look up at the clouds,
the sun slightly piercing through;
in the beauty of the heavens
I can see God move, too.

I can see Him move;
He transforms Himself in the sky
as He walks by, I can feel His
skirt of love brush over me.

He walks by me every morning, and before
I lay down to sleep at night, He winks at me.

And I get happy, so delighted that that awesome
God thinks about me, all day and all night.

As I ponder these thoughts in my mind,
I ask myself, "How long will it last?"

And God answers me,
**"for a lifetime, I promise.
A promise is a promise."**

"Remember, I gave you an Eternal Promise - MYSELF."

The Awesome Majesty of God

(interpretation of tongues)

Praise His name, Praise His name.
The Most High God, above everything
Both great and small.

Master of the universe, Ruler of the earth,
the mountains and the sea.

Great and Mighty King
Who sits upon the throne of mercy
And gives grace to help in time of need.

Such a gracious and wonderful Father is He,
Lord of all;
Tell me who or what can stand before thee;

For You created it. All things were created by You and for You, and without
You nothing was made that was made.

You are the Alpha, Omega, First, Last,
Beginning and End,
Which is, which was, and which is to come.

You are the Unexplainable, the Unpredictable, the Vindictive, the Rewarder,
the Infinite and Omniscient One, The Great I Am.
Who is likened unto thee?

"I AM God and besides Me there's not another."

I Feel You by My Side

Jesus, You are so beautiful to me;
your skin is so smooth, soft and perfectly sweet.

Your eyes are full of love,
they embrace me without consent.

Your arms are barrels of strength,
full of power and might.

Your hands are ever so tender,
I can't resist your healing touch.

Your lips are a well of water,
springing up into everlasting life.

Your voice thunders and
I'm awakened at your request;
my soul is mesmerized by its divine effect.

I follow the dance of your feet;
upon your step, I go where You go -
like Ruth and Naomi indeed.

Your hair smells like the fragrance
of rain on a light spring day;
I love You dear Lord, what more can I say.

While the heat of your passion awaits me,
I draw nearer to You, my Refuge and Strength.

In the warmth of your comfort,
in the breath of your love,
I laugh, I cry, I scream, I dream
about You because I feel You by my side.

You are My Sunshine

When I wake up in the morning,
the sun graciously poised is
proof enough that God exist
and without Him, we're just a mist.

When I wake up in the morning
a little song is in my heart
to sing to Him that I love Him.

My mind knocks on the door of my heart,
and it answers the call with gladness
right from the very start.

Joy moves my lips to whisper:
"Dear Jesus I love You, You're a friend of mine;
You supply my every need, my hungry soul You feed; I'm aware You are my
source, which all blessings flow; and with this thought in mind,
I know just where, where to go."

Yes, this is happening quite often,
more than I'd ever dream or expect.

This romance is priceless,
you just can't get it any other way -
that is, by loving Him with your
whole heart, soul, mind and strength.

A Letter of Thanks

As I'm sipping on a cup of tea,
looking out the window towards the sky,
my mind reflects on this semester ending.

I just want to say "thank you"
for being there for me.
When I got tired, You were my strength;
You have been my comfort.

You have made me what I am.
If it were not for You,
I couldn't smile the way I do;
if it were not for You,
I couldn't say the things I say;
if it were not for You,
I wouldn't know the things I know.

No one is strong enough to take your place;
thank you for being my help,
for being my friend.

Thank you for understanding my heart,
for holding me in the middle of the night.

Thank you for whispering in my ear -
for visiting me; your presence I cherish
and hold so dear.

Thank you for teaching me and holding my hand.
There are no words to express my gratitude
and appreciation, just tears of joy.

But if You can read tears,
I have a whole lot to say, and that is
"thank you" from beginning to end.

I don't know what the future holds for us,
but I thank you for this moment in time;

for You have been my Help and Strength -
a true friend of mine.

Obsessed by your Love

(To my Dearest Friend and Lover, Jesus)

I sit here idly, wondering if there's
any way possible to physically pursue
or experience your touch.

My urge to find You and smother You
with hugs and kisses drives me
to my knees to lay at your feet.

To feel your healing touch come over my body,
captivates my thoughts and sends a rushing
heavenly sensation to behold.

I have become this crazy woman for You;
no one's bothering me, but yet I sit here
and tears stream down my face.

While searching for some valid reason to explain
my reaction to the unknown, I ask myself,
"what in the world is wrong with me!?"

I try honestly, I do try to hold myself together,
but your love, Lord, won't let me go.

Yes, I blame your love,
for it is the most pleasant and sweetly
surprising experience life holds.

When the very inkling of a thought emerges
in my mind about my Savior,
my heart faints in gratitude,
helplessly trying to express
appreciation untold.

O, my soul pants after Thee,
for I am as the deer;
my desire is toward your

unfailing love for me.

I am simply obsessed to find You to love You back.

An Inspirational Thought for Valentine's Day

I hope you enjoy your day and experience
the love of God in a fresh, new way.

The brightness of His countenance
beams with expectation for you;
His romance is what we really seek for
without even knowing.

So let the Blessed Savior touch you
and fill you with His joy.

O, He'll sweep you off your feet,
If you'll embrace Him each day,
more and more.

You are My Dream

As I lay across my bed this morning,
I think about how good You've been to me.

I'm dreaming that if I could create
a rose garden, each pedal would say
in its own special way,
"thank you" for your tender mercies
are renewed every day;
great is thy faithfulness.

From your body,
I can feel the heat of your words;
they energize me, they electrify me,
they soothe me, they hold me and rock me
gently in the cradle of your love.

Your Word unlocks the door of my heart
and in my ear an echo whispers,
"we shall never depart;
come closer to me,
my sweet lovely dream."

What You do best, and that is LOVE,
is my response to your call.

I open myself up for your touch,
there are no boundaries between us.

Relaxing in your presence,
You come in and find a lodging place
to rest in my soul,
to have sweet communion
with me is where You abode.

And in Him, I find a love that has no end - everlasting love.

You are my dream come true; I love You.